Exploring New Roles for Librarians:

The Research Informationist

Synthesis Lectures on Emerging Trends in Librarianship

This series, ***Emerging Trends in Librarianship*** (a sub-series of the Synthesis Lectures on Library Science and Librarianship), will focus on new and emerging trends in digital collections and new technologies as they relate to the practice of librarianship and library science. The series will be of interest not only to librarians and information professionals, but also to the research community in general. Topics include but are not limited to: eScience, institutional repositories, data curation, advances in discovery tools, taxonomy and thesauri construction, mobile technologies, and the newest topic of "near field communication."

Editor

Hema Ramachandran, *California State University, Long Beach*

Joe Murphy, *Librarian and Technology Trend Analyst*

Exploring New Roles for Librarians: The Research Informationist
Lisa Federer
2014

Exploring New Roles for Librarians: The Research Informationist
Lisa Federer
www.morganclaypool.com

ISBN: 9781627052498 print
ISBN: 9781627052504 ebook

DOI 10.2200/S00570ED1V01Y201403ETL001

A Publication in the Morgan & Claypool Publishers series
SYNTHESIS LECTURES ON EMERGING TRENDS IN LIBRARIANSHIP #1
Series Editor: Hema Ramachandran, California State University, Long Beach; Joe Murphy, Librarian and Technology Trend Analyst

Series ISSN [COMING] Print [COMING] Electronic

Exploring New Roles for Librarians:

The Research Informationist

Lisa Federer

UCLA

SYNTHESIS LECTURES ON EMERGING TRENDS IN LIBRARIANSHIP #1

ABSTRACT

Librarians have been providing support to researchers for many years, typically with a focus on responding to researchers' needs for access to the existing literature. However, librarians' skills and expertise make them uniquely suited to provide a wide range of assistance to researchers across the entire research process, from conception of the research question to archiving of collected data at the project's conclusion. In response to increasingly stringent demands on researchers to share their data, and as computationally intensive and primarily data-driven scientific methods begin to take the place of traditional lab-based research, the "research informationist" has emerged as a new information profession. With a background in library and information sciences, as well as expertise in best practices for data management, grant funder policies, and informatics tools, the research informationist is capable of implementing a full suite of research support services. This book will discuss how the research informationist role has developed out of the previously established clinical informationist model and how it expands on the model of embedded librarianship. The book will also examine core competencies for the successful research informationist and the training and preparation necessary for students in library and information sciences programs, as well as currently practicing librarians. Finally, this book will consider how research informationists can form collaborative partnerships with research teams and build their services outside the walls of the library, citing practical examples of the types of support research informationists can offer.

KEYWORDS

research informationist, informationist, embedded librarian, data management, data curation, research data life cycle, eScience, eResearch, data literacy instruction

Contents

Acknowledgments

I am very grateful to my editor Hema Ramachandran, who caught me entirely off guard (in a good way) when she called and suggested I write this book. My thanks also to Diane Cerra and the rest of the staff at Morgan & Claypool for their assistance and patience along the way.

I owe a great debt of gratitude to my UCLA family, who helped shape the librarian I am today, especially Rikke Ogawa, Adele Dobry, Julie Kwan, Russell Johnson, and Lise Snyder. Their mentorship and friendship have been invaluable. I am particularly grateful to my director Judy Consales for supporting me in all my wild ideas and grand schemes; without her encouragement, I could not have accomplished much of the work I have described here.

The National Library of Medicine's administrative supplement for informationists helped lay the foundation for much of my early work in this field. I am extremely honored to have received one of these awards and have had the great pleasure to learn alongside some very talented informationists who also received this award. Many thanks to Dr. Zachary Taylor, who spent a lot of time teaching me about all sorts of things, like lasers and corneal hydration, and to the principal investigator of the funded project, Dr. Warren Grundfest.

Finally, I am endlessly grateful to my family for their support and love, as well as to Ali Sabzevari, who has been the most patient and loving friend anyone could ever hope to meet. And although she cannot read, it would be completely out of character for me not to thank Ophelia, my little four-legged buddy.

CHAPTER 1

Introduction

Libraries have existed in some form since the dawn of recorded knowledge, but as information and the ways that people access it have changed, libraries have transformed to meet users' evolving needs and preferences. Card catalogs gave way to online public access catalogs (OPACs), print journal subscriptions were replaced by electronic subscriptions, and microform and microfiche readers disappeared to make room for computer terminals. It is not only the physical spaces of libraries that must be remade to satisfy their users; librarians must also be responsive to the shifting landscape of information needs. The last several decades have seen widespread adoption of a variety of novel services to provide service to users whenever and wherever their information need arises. Some new services are logical extensions of existing services, such as moving traditional reference service to an online chat format, while others are substantive changes to the fundamental roles of librarianship. This book discusses one such emerging model of evolving roles in librarianship: the research informationist.

1.1 WHAT IS A RESEARCH INFORMATIONIST?

At the most basic level, a research informationist can be defined as an embedded information professional who provides specialized services to researchers at their point of need, such as in a laboratory or clinical research setting. These specialized services may include a variety of activities spanning the research life cycle, including expert searching, data curation (defined broadly as the various activities required to preserve data for reuse on a long-term basis), and guidance on scholarly communications. Most research informationists hold a master's degree in library and information studies from an American Library Association (ALA)-accredited institution; some also have additional training in a discipline relevant to the field in which they provide services, such as a bachelor's degree or second master's degree in a science.

As with many emerging roles, the research informationist role does not yet have a single consistent definition, and the services a research informationist provides may differ widely from one library to another. Chapter 2 will further discuss the evolution of the research informationist role and its context within traditional and evolving library services.

1.2 THE ROLE OF THE RESEARCH INFORMATIONIST IN THE 21ST CENTURY LIBRARY

A report on the Roundtable on Technology and Change in Academic Libraries organized in 2006 by the Association of College and Research Libraries (ACRL) defined the purpose of the research library as "not just to collect, but also to organize, preserve, and make knowledge accessible" (Association of College and Research Libraries, 2006). However, the forms that knowledge takes have multiplied and shifted in the 21st century, with the rise of the Internet and other new technologies that have revolutionized the ways that people communicate. The research informationist role reflects one way that libraries have begun to address the changing nature of knowledge and the challenges that face users in an age when information is ubiquitous and sometimes overwhelming.

Technology has not only changed how scientific researchers access information, but also fundamentally altered the ways that science is conducted. Computer scientist Jim Gray describes a "fourth paradigm" of science, in which scientific inquiry has become increasingly data-driven, relying less on simple observation and more on simulation, study of large-scale datasets, and other technologically supported means of analyzing information to gain a better understanding of complex phenomena (Gray, 2009). This data-driven science is also increasingly team based and interdisciplinary, with scientists from different subject backgrounds bringing their expertise to bear on complex questions through analysis of networked datasets.

As the ways that science is practiced evolve, so too do the information needs of those engaged in research, underscoring the need for information professionals with specialized expertise to help researchers navigate the vast universe of available information. Google and other search engines give users the perception that information is easily available at hand, but such resources often fail to adequately answer researchers' questions, and it can become time-consuming to manually sort through thousands of articles to find the one pearl they need. Information professionals with expertise to deliver relevant results can play an increasingly important role in the research enterprise.

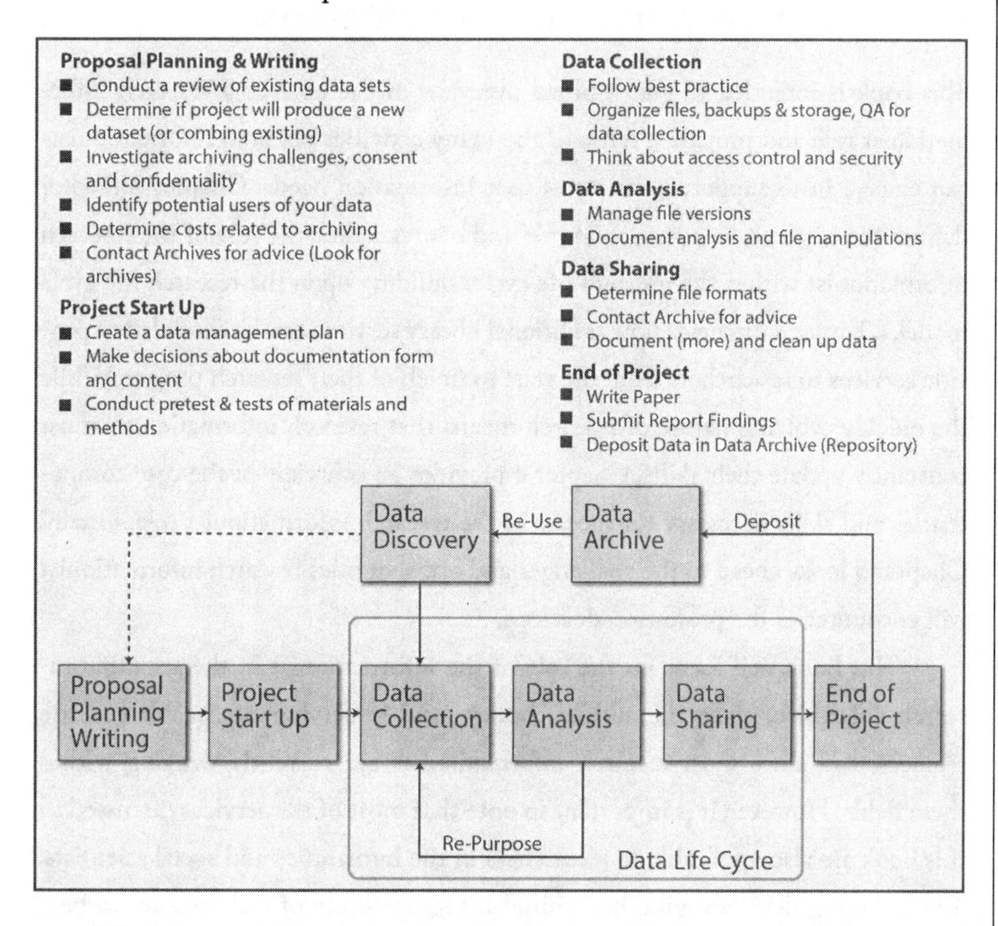

Steps in the Research Life Cycle. Based on Van den Eynden, et al. (2009, http://dmconsult.library.virginia.edu/lifecycle/).

Beyond their expertise in using bibliographic databases, information professionals also have a unique skillset that makes them ideally suited to support data-driven science. Such research by definition generates large amounts of data, but few researchers have the training or expertise to adequately manage such datasets. With their training in information-seeking behavior, organization and description of information, and digital preservation, information professionals can contribute to research by assisting researchers in managing and curating datasets that will be easier to analyze, share, and re-use.

1.3 SCOPE OF THIS BOOK'S DISCUSSION

This book is intended to give a broad overview of the emerging research informationist role and provide a sense of the many activities research informationists can engage in to support a variety of user information needs. Chapter 2 further defines the research informationist role and contextualize the role of the research informationist within the research life cycle. Building upon the research life cycle model, Chapter 3 discusses how traditional library services can be extended to provide services to researchers from the start to finish of their research project. While the quickly evolving nature of research means that research informationists must constantly update their skills, Chapter 4 provides an overview of the core competencies and skills necessary for success in the research informationist role. Finally, Chapter 5 looks ahead to the challenges and opportunities research informationist will encounter as the profession develops.

This book will focus on the role of the informationist in the scientific research enterprise, given the author's background in serving the health and life sciences, and since most research informationists are currently working within these fields. However, it is important to note that most of the services discussed in this book are also applicable to researchers in the humanities and social scientists. The emerging field of digital humanities brings a variety of technologies to bear on humanities and social science research, and in turn creates problems around data management and scholarly communications similar to those that scientific researchers face. As more humanities and social sciences researchers begin to leverage new technologies to conduct novel types of scholarly research, informationist services will be increasingly relevant outside of the sciences.

CHAPTER 2

Embedded Librarianship and the Evolution of the Informationist Service Model

In 2011, the William H. Welch Medical Library at Johns Hopkins University announced that they would be closing their doors and moving all their services online. The decision was based in part on the overwhelmingly digital nature of their users' access: on an average day, Welch Library users downloaded 35,000 articles from online subscriptions, while only 40 people came to the library and checked out books (Kelley, 2011).

Although the Welch Library ultimately revisited their plan and decided to keep their physical spaces, the notion of an entirely digital library with no physical space is not entirely radical in an age when many users look to the Internet, not to the library, for their information needs. The 2012 Ithaka S+R U.S. Faculty Survey demonstrates a clear preference among higher education faculty to access digital sources as opposed to visiting the library. Fewer than 5% of respondents viewed the library building as their preferred starting point for conducting research. Hardly any of the respondents said that they would ask a librarian for help with beginning their research process. At the same time, 80% of respondents considered their college or university library's collections and subscriptions "very important" in accessing materials for research and teaching, more than any other source (Housewright et al., 2013).

If users need library information but won't come to the library, one solution is to bring the library to the users. E-books and online subscriptions make the library's collections accessible wherever the user is, but many of the other services that libraries provide rely on librarians who can interact with users; thus, many libraries have started sending their librarians out to their users. Research informationists have evolved out of this outreach model to provide expert services within the setting of the users' place of work.

2.1 EMBEDDED LIBRARIANSHIP

Given that many resources that researchers, students, and other users need are available in digital form, accessible from almost anywhere, it has become entirely feasible for a user to complete his or her research project without ever setting foot in a library. However, a library is not just a building with many books and journals in it—the library offers services that make research easier and enhance the user experience. Perhaps one of the most important resources in the research library is the reference librarian, who can guide users to information, teach them how to use bibliographic databases, and help give them the skills they need to be lifelong learners.

If online resources bring information to users at the place and time they need it, why not take the librarian out of the library and send him or her to that place? This is the idea behind "embedded librarianship," a term inspired by the concept of embedding journalists with troops during the war in Iraq (Dewey, 2004). As online distance education gained in popularity, some librarians became embedded with specific courses by incorporating information literacy instruction within the online course, making library materials available on the course website, participating in the class's online discussion forum, and offering online chat reference service (Kearly and Phillips, 2004; Matthew and Schroeder, 2006).

As new technology becomes available, embedded librarians have moved into these spaces to provide reference and instruction to the users where they need it. Many libraries give their users the opportunity to connect with a reference librarian remotely through email, instant messaging, or live chat. Librarians answer reference questions that users direct to the library on Twitter, a social networking and microblogging tool (Fields, 2010). Librarians even provide reference services in virtual spaces, like Second Life, an online virtual world where users interact with each other through avatars (Grassian and Trueman, 2007).

Librarians continue to explore new spaces, both real and virtual, where they can become embedded to provide services to users. Some librarians are embedded with in-person courses, not just showing up once for a single library instruction session, but attending every class and becoming a participant in the class. Working so closely with the students gives the librarian visibility and credibility among the students, and also gives him or her a better understanding of the context of the class and assignments, so as to provide better reference service (Hall, 2008). Embedded librarianship services continue to evolve, with an emphasis on embedded librarians gaining specific subject knowledge, building relationships with their users, and providing specialized information and other value-added services that help expand the importance and relevance of the library (Shumaker and Tally, 2010).

2.2 THE CLINICAL INFORMATIONIST

Around the same time that academic reference librarians were exploring opportunities to become embedded with their users, medical libraries also began sending their librarians out to the spaces where their users worked. The term "informationist" was coined in 2000 to refer to information professionals who worked within the clinical team (Davidoff and Florance, 2000). However, their view of an informationist was as an entirely new profession, rather than a form of embedded librarianship. In fact, they even envisioned an entirely new training program and method of certification. The informationist would need training in both the clinical sciences as well as library and information studies. One might enter the field as a doctor or nurse who went on to undertake courses in information studies, or as a librarian who took additional studies in medicine. The informationist would thus be prepared to participate as a fully recognized member of the clinical team, working in a hospital or other clinical setting.

At the time of the Davidoff and Florance article, some medical librarians felt that they already did the work that the article described, as demonstrated vividly in the title of one such article: "'The informationist: a new health profession?' So what are we? Chopped liver?" (Kronenfeld, 2000). In letters to the editor of the

Annals of Internal Medicine in response to the Davidoff and Florance article, physicians argued that they could (or at least should be able to) retrieve the relevant literature themselves (Houghton and Rich, 2001; Sandroni, 2001). Nonetheless, many hospitals have recognized the importance of the informationist as a member of the clinical team, and a body of literature in medical librarianship has addressed the best ways of preparing professionals to serve in these roles and explorations of new opportunities for informationists. A decade after Davidoff and Florance's article, many hospitals faced with severe budget cuts are closing their libraries, making it more important than ever for librarians to demonstrate their value and explore new ways of serving their users.

2.3 THE RESEARCH INFORMATIONIST IN THE SCIENCES

Drawing on the clinical informationist model and the concept of embedded librarianship, the research informationist has emerged as an information professional who serves researchers at their point of need, often working within laboratory and clinical research settings. Like their clinical counterparts, research informationists usually have training in both library and information studies and the field of the researchers to whom they provide services. Most research informationist programs have developed in the sciences, particularly the health sciences, although researchers in other fields, particularly the digital humanities, could benefit from the assistance of a research informationist. Research informationists may have advanced degrees in a science, but many do not have formal training. Regardless of their formal background in the sciences, continuing education is crucial for research informationists, in much the same way as it is for physicians and other health professionals; with scientific knowledge expanding so quickly, staying up to date with the current state of the field is essential for the successful research informationist.

Besides being embedded within research settings, research informationists also provide a variety of services that expand on the traditional librarian role. Frequently, library services focus on the "last mile" of research—collecting the scholarly literature and helping users get access to it. However, research informationists provide services across the entire research life cycle, from start to finish.

The research life cycle typically begins with the development of a research question, frequently drawing on the existing literature to inform the question and how it will be answered. The research informationist can assist with searching for the literature, as well as participating in formal literature searches, such as systematic reviews and meta-analyses. As researchers prepare their funding proposals to earn grant funding to undertake their research, research informationists can assist with developing a data management plan, a new requirement for many funders. Once the research begins, the research informationist can advise on proper data management and assist in addressing questions that arise by referring to the scientific literature. When researchers are prepared to share their findings, research informationists can answer copyright questions and help researchers ensure that the copyright transfer agreements they sign allow them the right to deposit their article in an open access repository like PubMed Central, if their grant funder requires them to do so. Even after the research project is complete, researchers still must be stewards of their data, and research informationists can help with preservation and curation of the data, such as by migrating formats as technology evolves. Research informationists can also help researchers track the impact of their work through bibliometrics, which use metrics like citation counts to quantify the influence or importance of a scholar's work, and emerging measures of impact referred to as "altmetrics" that examine the dissemination of a scholar's work across social media like Twitter, Facebook, and Mendeley.

Frequently, research informationists function as members of the research team, which may include a primary investigator (PI), research scientists, postdoctoral fellows, and graduate and undergraduate students. Research informationists often attend meetings of the research team, and many are present in the lab where research is conducted. Just as the embedded librarian who attends each class can provide more informed assistance to the students, the research informationist who spends time in the lab has a better understanding of the research team's work and also gains credibility.

Research informationists also have a role in the research team as instructors of information and data literacy. Very few academic science programs teach their students data management; it is assumed that they will learn these practices hands-on from their mentors as they work in labs. However, these more senior scientists have rarely received any formal training in data management either, and instead have developed ad hoc practices for lab organization. While some labs follow good data management practices, many do not, such as by failing to back up their data on a regular basis or naming their files and coding their data in ways that make sense to them but would be impossible for others to understand. Research informationists who spend time in the lab have an opportunity to provide on-the-spot instruction to the research team on best practices for data management. Working with students in the lab is particularly important in helping to create a new generation of scientists who are trained in proper techniques for managing their data.

Research informationists are especially important at this particular juncture in scientific inquiry, as scientists are increasingly overwhelmed by the "data deluge." Technology has advanced to the point that information can be collected in novel ways never before possible, resulting in large datasets that must be curated and prepared for analysis. For example, scientists have developed sensors small enough to be carried on a bee's back, and the Commonwealth Scientific and Industrial Research Organisation has fit 5,000 Australian bees with sensors that will track their movement (Commonwealth Scientific and Industrial Research Organisation, 2014). Public health researchers have begun to use the vast amount of information in Twitter for biosurveillance, such as tracking influenza epidemics and drug abuse. Twitter users generate 400 million tweets every single day, and the Library of Congress had collected more than 170 billion tweets as of October 2012, amounting to 133.2 terabytes of data (Kessler, 2013). As of January 2014, the Library of Congress has not made these tweets available to the public because they still haven't figured out a way to make such a huge dataset manageable. Many researchers face the same dilemma—what is the best way to manage and analyze such massive datasets?

In particular, the set of biomedical fields known collectively as the "omics," such as genomics, proteomics, and transcriptomics, by their nature generate a great deal of data. Researchers in these fields mine large datasets from many individuals to understand the structure and function of parts of organisms or systems. Once prohibitively expensive for most researchers, whole genome sequencing has become quicker and cheaper, making it possible for more labs to map the complete genome sequence of individual humans and other organisms. Genome wide association studies (GWAS) look at the genome sequences of tens or even hundreds of thousands of individuals in hopes of identifying the genetic basis for disease or other traits. With an individual human genome sequence taking up several gigabytes of storage space, it is clear that genomics researchers are indeed facing a data deluge as they continue to gather more sequences (Zhao, et al., 2013).

Librarians who take on research informationist roles have training in organizing information and can be a valuable asset to research teams of all kinds, whether they are "Big Data" researchers or small labs with more modest datasets. With a research informationist to assist with data organization and curation, researchers will be able to analyze their data more efficiently and effectively.

CHAPTER 3

Research Informationist Services Across the Research Life Cycle

Although the types of assistance that research informationists render may seem like novel offerings, these services are a logical extension of the libraries' traditional offerings. The skills and knowledge that librarians have been bringing to their work since the days of the first libraries applies to information in almost any form it may take, even now that we have entered a digital age. Although the unit of information is different—datasets of various types—the research informationist's services in many ways mirror the tasks that his or her colleagues apply to books, journals, maps, or other materials, both digital and analog.

3.1 THE DATA REFERENCE INTERVIEW

The reference interview is one of the most essential skills that a successful reference librarian must master. Experienced reference librarians recognize that the question a patron asks may not reflect the patron's true information need for a variety of different reasons, including the patron's lack of adequate background information, misconceptions about reference services, or unfamiliarity with available resources. The terms "reference interview" and "reference transaction" both capture the cooperative nature of reference activities; the American Library Association's Reference and User Services Association's definition of reference also reflects the active role of the librarian, who must "interpret" and "evaluate," rather than merely answer, a reference question (Reference and User Services Association, 2008). The patron's true information need may be quite different from the originally articulated question, so the effective reference librarian uses a variety of skills to elicit additional information from the patron, such as open-ended questioning, active listening, and verbal and non-verbal cues (Reference and User Services Association Task Force on Professional Competencies, 2003).

Likewise, the successful research informationist must master the technique of the "data reference interview." In fact, the negotiation of the researcher's information need is perhaps even more crucial for the research informationist because most researchers have very little awareness of the kind of services the research informationist can provide. Even more important, many researchers do not recognize the areas in which their own data management practices fall short. For example, many researchers do not adequately back up their data, are unfamiliar with the concept of controlled vocabularies, and do not describe their data with ease of use by others I mind. Because they were never instructed in best practices for data management, they are likely unaware that they could be working more effectively, and even less likely to realize that a research informationist is someone who could help with these needs. The cooperative nature of the traditional reference interview is highlighted in the data reference interview: the researcher and the informationist each bring their own unique expertise to the encounter, and the successful disposition of the question relies equally on both individuals.

Given the many types of data and many different fields of research that a research informationist may encounter, the exact format of the data reference interview will likely vary from one researcher to the next. However, the effective data reference interview should broadly assess the researchers' data and the institutional and discipline-specific cultures in which those data reside. Ideally, such an assessment would happen at the location where the data is stored or collected so that the research informationist can see actual examples of the data, and would address the data across the entire research life cycle, considering such questions as follows:

- In what format(s) is the data collected, and why was this format(s) selected?
- What type of metadata or additional information would another researcher with expertise in the field of study need in order to understand how this data was gathered, analyzed, or used?

- Do community standards exist for data description (such as controlled vocabularies or ontologies) and data sharing (such as repositories) within the discipline or field of study?

- Does the dataset contain personally identifiable information (PII) that makes it subject to additional security and privacy constraints?

- How long will data be retained after the end of the study, and what measures will need to be taken to ensure its continued viability (such as format migration)?

The Purdue University Libraries' Data Curation Profiles (http://datacurationprofiles.org/) is a useful resource for research informationists who would like to learn more about conducting data reference interviews, as well as documentation of the data practices of researchers in a variety of scientific fields (Purdue University Libraries, 2012). Depending on the point in the research life cycle of the project, as well as the research informationist's own skills and expertise, the research data interview will help the informationist and the researcher identify the strengths and weaknesses of existing data strategies in order to plan the most effective strategies for collaboration moving forward.

The data reference interview may involve not only addressing a researcher's data needs, but may also require the informationist to assist the researcher in finding an existing dataset. Just as reference librarians are aware of the key reference works and authoritative texts within their fields, such as the *Diagnostic and Statistical Manual* (DSM) for psychology or *Harrison's Principles of Internal Medicine*, research informationists should be aware of major repositories and sources of datasets. With greater emphasis by funding agencies on data sharing and with budgets becoming tighter, data re-use can be an efficient method for conducting research. While the universe of available datasets is far too vast for any one individual to commit to memory, research informationists should be aware of major repositories in fields relevant to their patrons' research, as well as indices of discipline-specific repositories, such as Databib (http://databib.org/), which catalogs over 600 repositories in a wide variety of subject areas (Databib, 2013).

3.2 DATA LITERACY INSTRUCTION

In an ideal world, a research informationist would have the time to individually consult with every researcher who needs help with their data management practices to help create an institution where every lab gathered data that was well organized and prepared to share should the need arise. Realistically, of course, given the constraints of budgets and time, a research informationist can hope to provide in-depth services to only a small fraction of the institution's patrons. Thus, data literacy instruction is an essential aspect of research informationists' services. Conducting classes allows the informationist to reach a much larger audience with a small investment of time compared to if the informationist consulted with each attendee individually.

The Association of College & Research Libraries defines information literacy as "the set of skills needed to find, retrieve, analyze, and use information" (Association of College and Research Libraries, 2014). Traditional information literacy instruction focuses on teaching students how to be information literate so that they are confident in their ability to independently address their own information needs. In the same sense, an individual who is data literate has learned the skills to gather, organize, describe, analyze, preserve, and share data.

Data literacy instruction is especially important for students who will go on to conduct research themselves. Few academic programs offer specific training in data management; most students learn about data management from their research mentors, who also did not receive such training. Thus, many scientific labs use ad-hoc, locally developed systems for managing and tracking their data in the lab, if they have any system at all. Teaching good data management practices to students who will become the next generation of principal investigators is crucial in ensuring that data will be viable and useful moving forward.

The exact form that data literacy instruction takes may differ from one institution to the next, depending on the needs and the existing knowledge of the researchers at the institution, as well as institutional requirements regarding data management. Some libraries offer a one-shot, broad introduction to data management, often focused around the research data life cycle model. Other institutions offer workshops that discuss specific data management topics in greater depth, such as how to write a data management plan or how to prepare datasets for sharing.

A number of curricula are available to guide informationists in the development of a data literacy instruction program at their institution, such as the Frameworks for a Data Management Curriculum (http://library.umassmed.edu/data_management_frameworks.pdf) developed at Lamar Soutter Library at the University of Massachusetts Medical School, and the George C. Gordon Library at Worcester Polytechnic Institute (Lamar Soutter Library, University of Massachusetts Medical School and the George C. Gordon Library, Worcester Polytechnic Institute, 2012). While these curricula are an excellent jumping-off point for the informationist wishing to develop a course of instruction, it is crucial to consider how to best adapt the broad recommendations to the needs of patrons at the institution. For example, does the institution have an institutional repository (IR) where articles are datasets can be shared? Are there resources like REDCap (Research Electronic Data Capture) (http://project-redcap.org/) or other data management tools available to researchers at the institution?

Another consideration in the development of a data literacy instruction curriculum is the method of delivery. Traditionally, information literacy instruction has been drop-in, in-person classes held in the library at a given time. However, by the nature of their work, researchers have a variety of time constraints that may make it difficult for them to come to the library for a class. Thus, informationists should consider alternative modes of delivery to ensure that researchers can get the information they need at the time they need it. Depending on the technology available at the institution, it may be possible to offer hybrid webinar/in-person courses, webinars, presentations in the researchers' labs, archived recorded instructional sessions, or even short online tutorials that cover a specific question. The key to success for a data literacy instruction series is ensuring that the informationist is delivering the information that researchers need in the best way for them to receive it, so a campaign of data literacy instruction must begin with careful consideration of the factors that may affect attendance and interest in such classes.

More importantly, data literacy instruction should include some assessment component to ensure that classes are meeting researchers' needs and expectations and to elicit suggestions about future topics researchers would like to see covered in workshops. Simple post-class evaluations require little time or effort to administer but can yield crucial information that will help in tailoring and improving data literacy offerings.

3.3 DATA DESCRIPTION, ORGANIZATION, AND CURATION

Jorge Luis Borges' short story "The Library of Babel" describes an infinite library full of books arranged in no apparently meaningful order, and the men who spend their entire lives searching the library for some meaning. Some of these men yearn to find "book which is the formula and perfect compendium *of all the rest*" while others "maintain that nonsense is normal in the Library and that the reasonable (and even humble and pure coherence) is an almost miraculous exception" (Borges, 2007). In many ways, the current state of e-research and data intensive science is not unlike Borges' Library. Researchers may organize their datasets or name their files in a way that makes sense to them, but would mean little to a colleague. New connections between researchers that could lead to fruitful collaborations go unmade because neither has described their dataset in a way that makes sense to the other. Standards and file formats change, making some datasets useless because the technology to access them no longer exists. As the amount of data available to researchers increases, so too does the need to remain that is organized, described, and preserved. Cataloging, indexing, and maintaining collections are all traditional library functions that translate well to the world of data management.

Informationists can assist with organization and description at multiple levels. First, elements within the data should be described with adequate metadata; for example, where was this sample collected and what does the abbreviation AuC stand for? Datasets themselves should also be described, especially if they will be sent to a repository, so that other researchers have a clear idea of what the dataset contains. Most importantly, informationists should advise researchers on how to use controlled vocabularies that are appropriate to their data and their community of practice. Using their knowledge of information seeking behavior, it may also be informative for the informationist to work backwards in determining what terms might be used to describe a dataset: if I were a researcher looking for this dataset, where would I look and what kind of terms would I search for?

The process of describing and organizing data can be time-consuming, particularly when the researcher has a large backlog of research materials. However, this work ultimately benefits the researcher by making his or her data easier to find and also creates the potential for collaboration with other researchers in their field or interdisciplinary research. With an increased emphasis on interdisciplinary research, adequate description of datasets is especially crucial. Having an informationist who is not as familiar with the data as the research team may actually be useful; while the research team has come to see their data as being useful for a specific purpose, the informationist's broader perspective on science may allow him or her to provide advice on how to make the dataset more collaboration-ready.

3.4 SCHOLARLY COMMUNICATION AND DATA SHARING

Traditional academic library services do not end once the researcher's manuscript is completed. Librarians with expertise in copyright can provide valuable help to authors in negotiating copyright agreements with publishers. Recently, librarians have also begun to assist authors in ensuring that they are compliant with the National Institutes of Health's Public Access Policy, which requires that authors deposit grant-funded articles in PubMed Central, the NIH open access repository (National Institutes of Health, 2013). In the academic environment, where researchers are concerned with tenure and promotion, librarians also assist researchers in demonstrating the impact of their scholarship through bibliometrics.

Informationists provide many of these services as well, but can also assist with the disposition of the data once the project is complete. Although the peer-reviewed journal article is generally considered the final product of research, the data gathered in the course of conducting this research is as important, if not more so, than the article. These data can be essential for reproducibility, a crucial problem in science, and also have the potential to be re-used by other researchers in novel ways. The National Science Foundation recognized the importance of datasets in their 2012 Proposal and Award Policies and Procedures Guide, which replaced the "Publications" section of the applicant Biosketch with a "Products" section, which could include datasets as well as publications (National Science Foundation, 2012).

Informationists can play a key role in helping researchers not only share their data, but receive credit for doing so, which is crucial in the competitive research world. First, informationists should be aware of the many different levels and methods of sharing. Many researchers are hesitant to share their datasets because of the incorrect assumption that this means making their datasets completely open to the public. In fact, many methods of sharing exist, including more secure methods, such as data enclaves, that are appropriate for sensitive datasets that may include personally identifiable information (PII). As federal funders increasingly call for grantees to share their data, informationists can play a key role in educating researchers on how to share their data appropriately.

Getting credit for shared data is also essential. Citing an article, book, or other source is standard practice in scholarly writing, and indeed, not doing so can be considered serious misconduct. However, citing datasets can be more difficult because of the lack of standards for doing so. Organizations like DataCite are working on this problem, but informationists can also assist at the local level. For example, informationists can facilitate the process of obtaining a digital object identifier (DOI) for a researcher's dataset, which will provide a persistent link back to the data and an easy method for citing it. A number of "data journals" exist, which accept submissions of datasets and provide a citation that looks much like that of a traditional journal, making it easier for future authors to cite the dataset. Although many researchers are currently reluctant to share their data, they will likely find themselves forced to do so by funder requirements, so informationists should work with researchers to dispel their misconceptions about sharing and assist in making the process of sharing as easy as possible.

CHAPTER 4

Core Competencies for Research Informationists

The evolving world of science calls for information professionals with a variety of skills and knowledge. Cutting edge researchers need the support of research informationists who are agile and have wide-ranging expertise across both information science and subjects specific to the discipline with which they work. The specific needs of individual research teams will likely vary widely based on team members' backgrounds and interests, but research informationists should at the minimum bring a certain set of basic core competencies to their work. This chapter takes a broad view on the types of skills and expertise that combine to make a successful research informationist. In addition to the specialized skills discussed here, a research informationist should also have the knowledge and expertise typically associated with traditional library service, such as those outlined in "Professional Competencies for Reference and User Services Librarians" (Reference and User Services Association Task Force on Professional Competencies, 2003).

4.1 RESEARCH PRINCIPLES AND PRACTICES

The activities that make a scientific project successful begin long before a researcher ever begins gather data and continues well after findings are reported in publication. The successful research informationist should understand the research life cycle and look for the points in that cycle at which his or her information expertise can supplement the researchers' scientific expertise. While researchers are intimately familiar with the scientific methods associated with their work, few have ever had formal training in planning for data management, negotiating copyright transfer agreements, and other topics that often fall within the purview of the informationist's background and expertise. Thus, informationists should familiarize themselves with the requirements that researchers will need to meet in order to provide guidance.

The research process often begins with the preparation of a grant proposal. Although most researchers have experience with writing proposals, many find themselves unsure of how to address new funder requirements that call for a data management plan (DMP) to accompany proposals for funding. For example, in January 2011, the National Science Foundation (NSF) began requiring all proposals to include a plan for how research data would be collected, managed, and preserved (National Science Foundation, 2011). A similar policy from the National Institutes of Health (NIH) calls for all proposals seeking more than $500,000 in direct funding per year to submit a plan for how they will share their final research data (National Institutes of Health, 2007). Online resources like the DMPTool (https://dmp.cdlib.org/) (University of California Curation Center, 2013) and the DMPonline (http://www.dcc.ac.uk/dmponline) (Digital Curation Centre, 2013) provide interactive templates to guide researchers through writing their DMP. While these tools offer an extremely valuable starting point for researchers who have never written a DMP, consultation with an informationist is even more valuable. The informationist can provide individualized suggestions based on the type of data the researcher is collecting, data storage and repository services that may be appropriate for the deposit of final data, and other institution-specific guidance.

Besides being familiar with best practices in data management, research informationists should also make an effort to learn about the specific of data management within the fields that their users conduct research. Many areas of research have community-based standards that allow researchers within the field to communicate their results with their colleagues more efficiently and facilitate reproducibility of experiments. For example, the Minimum Information About a Microarray Experiment (MIAME) standard outlines six elements that all researchers should describe in their publications (Functional Genomics Data Society, 2010). Other fields may have metadata standards that researchers will be expected to use to describe their datasets, such as the Ecological Metadata Language (EML) that is the standard for documenting ecological data (The Knowledge Network for

Biocomplexity, n.d.). Some such standards are so ubiquitous in their respective fields that researchers will already be aware of them, but for fields that are still developing standards, the informationist may be able to provide guidance that will help shape how researchers organize their data.

The process of sharing data may also differ from one field to the next. Informationists should be sensitive to the fact that researchers in some communities consider data sharing standard practice, while others may not be as open to sharing their data. Tenopir et al.'s study of researchers' attitudes toward data sharing reveals wide variations based on a variety of factors, including geographic region, age, and subject discipline (Tenopir, et al., 2011).

In addition to sharing final research data, some researchers are required by their funders to make the articles arising from grant funding publically available through an open access repository. Such is the case for all NIH grantees, who must make their articles available in PubMed Central in accordance with the NIH Public Access Policy (National Institutes of Health, 2013). Some colleges and universities, including the University of California, have also instituted policies requiring their faculty to make their work available in an institutional repository (University of California , 2013). Although many researchers agree with the spirit of making their scholarship more widely available, compliance with such policies can be a complex and multi-step process.

Informationists can be of valuable assistance with complying with these policies. First, informationists should have some basic knowledge of copyright law in order to assist researchers in ensuring that copyright transfer agreements they sign with journals allow them to deposit the articles within the embargo period that the policy requires. Additionally, researchers may need advice about how to submit to a repository as well as which repositories may be appropriate for submission when one is not specifically named by the policy. Informationists should also maintain familiarity with the quickly shifting field of open access publishing in general, as researchers may be interested in making their work more openly available even when not required to do so.

4.2 SPECIALIZED INFORMATION RESOURCES

Most librarians have enough experience with literature searching that they can generally find their way around even when presented with a bibliographic database they've never used before. However, bibliographic databases are not the only information resources that researchers use in their daily work. Researchers in many fields rely on specialized databases containing information such as chemical structures, genetic sequences, and other types of data. Informationists should familiarize themselves with the information resources that may be applicable to researchers they assist.

It may not be feasible for informationists without a background in science to use these resources to the same extent that a well-versed researcher can. For example, searching in bioinformatics resources like GenBank requires a relatively high level of knowledge about genetics and sequencing (National Center for Biotechnology Information, 2013). However, informationists should at least familiarize themselves with what kinds of questions each resource can answer and any additional search features available, such as controlled vocabularies or ontologies used in the database, whether Boolean searches can be used, and whether specific fields are searchable. Many researchers do not use the full range of features available in a database, instead simply typing their query in natural language into the basic search box. While such simplistic searches may retrieve some information, consultation from an informationist who can provide guidance on use of advanced search features will likely yield more satisfying results.

Advances in technology also provide new and more powerful methods for searching the scientific literature. Resources that utilize semantic web and natural language processing technologies allow researchers to uncover previously unnoticed associations within a body of literature. For example, using a tool called Semantic MEDLINE, which summarizes MEDLINE citations using natural language processing, researchers may be able to use the existing scientific literature to realize previously unrecognized relationships that explain disease and suggest possibilities for treatment (Miller, et al., 2012). Similar technology applied to electronic health records can provide researchers the opportunity to collect information from virtual patient populations to conduct epidemiological research on a much larger scale than would ever be possible with traditional observational methods (Perlis et al., 2012). The complexity of language, particularly with regard to clinical text, makes natural language processing challenging, and most technology has not yet reached the point that text can be automatically interpreted with the necessary degree of accuracy. Informationists should remain aware of developments in these fields and related areas so as to be prepared to advise researchers of emerging technologies that may be of relevance to their work.

4.3 SUBJECT MATTER KNOWLEDGE

In their original article defining the clinical informationist, Davidoff and Florance recognize that clinical informationists may be either clinicians who undertake training in library and information studies, or established information professionals who go on to complete additional training in the clinical sciences (Davidoff and Florance, 2000). Although some research informationists do have previous training in a scientific field, even up to the level of a doctoral degree, formal education in the sciences is not necessarily a prerequisite for success as an informationist. In fact, researchers who focus closely on very specific niche areas of science may even benefit from the input of an informationist who does not have a particular disciplinary background and the assumptions that come along with such training.

While informationists can certainly succeed without a degree in a science, an awareness of the scientific method, research practices, and the principles of the science in which they work are a necessity. Without at least a basic understanding of the work that researchers are conducting, an informationist cannot effectively assess their information needs or advise on how to manage their data. Fortunately, for the motivated informationist, there are a variety of resources that can help them gain proficiency with the sciences. Purdue's Data Curation Profiles is a useful tool for gaining background knowledge about data and curation practices within a particular field of research. The website contains profiles for a number of different scientific fields, as well as a downloadable version of the "toolkit" that librarians and informationists can use to create and submit data curation profiles for disciplines not yet covered on the site (Purdue University Libraries, 2012).

The broad scope of competencies necessary for informationists' success underscores the importance of continuing education, but also the need to revisit the curriculum for the MLIS degree to ensure that ALA-accredited programs are creating information professionals with the skills needed to support scientific research. The next chapter will discuss how the research informationist role may bring change to librarian education as well as the delivery of library and information services in the profession.

CHAPTER 5

Conclusions

In an age when digital communication provides instant access to a whole world of information, libraries and librarians must evolve to remain relevant and meet the changing needs of their users. Most importantly, librarians must recognize that they cannot wait for their users to come to them—they must go to their users and make a compelling case for what the library can do for the users. The traditional tasks of the academic library must continue—reference services, maintaining the collection, cataloging and organizing information, and preserving valuable intellectual and cultural resources—but the 21st century library must also find new ways to engage their users and hire information professionals with the skills to do so.

5.1 IMPLICATIONS FOR LIBRARIAN EDUCATION

In the early 2000s, it was becoming apparent to many library school deans that the curricula of their programs needed to reflect the evolving landscape of digital information. In response, a group of library schools formed the "iSchools Caucus." These iSchools, or information schools, seek to educate their students on "the relationship between information, technology, and people" (iSchools, 2012). Many iSchools and other library schools have begun offering courses in data science, big data, and data analytics, which will help prepare the budding research informationist. A number of library schools even offer a specialization or certification in data science or big data. Students who emerge with their masters of library and information science degree with these specializations will likely be qualified many opportunities that their colleagues who have followed a more traditional course of library study do not.

Many library schools offer internships, practicums, or other field work that will give their students hands-on experience with the type of work that they may go on to do after they graduate, as well as connecting them with mentors. This type of real-world experience is extremely valuable for students interested in working in research informationist positions, particularly those who do not have a scientific background. Although the skills typically taught in library schools—describing and organizing information, conducting reference service, and teaching information literacy—lay a theoretical and practical framework, the successful research informationist needs a variety of other skills that are not taught in library schools.

Even with internships, does the MLIS alone adequately prepare students to work as research informationists? Davidoff and Florance argue that the clinical informationist needs education in both information studies and clinical science. Nonetheless, there are many successful clinical informationists working today who do not have formal education in clinical science. Given that research informationist is an emerging role, it is likely too soon to define the exact education that is necessary, as well as whether this education should differ significantly from the typical MLIS. As the responsibilities of research informationists evolve and become consistent, so too may the educational foundations required to fulfill those responsibilities. In the meantime, library schools should remain aware of new opportunities in the field, like research informationist, and adjust their curricula to educate their students accordingly.

5.2 IMPLICATIONS FOR DELIVERY OF LIBRARY SERVICES

With budget cuts becoming increasingly common and with many hospital libraries shuttering their doors for good, it is essential that libraries demonstrate their value. Providing research informationist services brings visibility to the library by sending an individual out into the spaces where users are doing their work. Research informationist services also help change users' perception of the library—rather than simply a place that holds books, the library provides valuable, cutting-edge services to solve problems for which users would not typically look to the library.

Research informationist services can also serve as a valuable source of funding, particularly important as library budgets shrink and expenses increase. The National Library of Medicine has provided administrative supplements for research informationists to join existing NIH-funded research teams (Florance, 2013). As awareness of the research informationist role increases among researchers, funding for research informationists may be written into grants as research team members. A research informationist working with grant-funded research teams could in theory fund his or her entire position through grants.

Libraries must seek out new opportunities for collaboration and create new relationships and alliances. Library directors should encourage their librarians to explore new opportunities and create an environment that fosters creativity and inventiveness. Librarians also must be willing to step outside of their usual roles and explore new venues in which their skills would be needed. Rather than viewing the changing information landscape as a threat, librarians should challenge themselves to look for new ways to use their expertise and engage with their users. The research informationist role is one way to do so, but librarians are also exploring new ideas like gamification (Kim, 2013), altmetrics (Priem et al., 2010), and geographical information systems (GIS) (ESRI, 2014), to name just a few.

As the ways that users find, access, and use information evolves, libraries must remain agile and respond to the changing needs of their users. One of the key points to remember in a reference interview is that the user may not be able to articulate or even be aware of his or her true information need. That same awareness should be brought to the development of new library services, addressing users' needs even if they are not aware that they had the need. Whether they are called librarians or informationists or something else entirely, information professionals must think about new ways to apply their skills and keep in mind their own advice to be lifelong learners.

Bibliography

Association of College and Research Libraries. (2014). *Introduction to Information Literacy*. Retrieved January 2, 2014, from Association of College & Research Libraries: http://www.ala.org/acrl/issues/infolit/overview/intro. 16

Association of College and Research Libraries. (2006). Changing Roles of Academic and Research Libraries. *Roundtable on Technology and Change in Academic Libraries*. American Library Association. 2

Borges, J. L. (2007). The Library of Babel. In J. L. Borges, *Labyrinths* (pp. 51-58). New York: New Directions. 18

Commonwealth Scientific and Industrial Research Organisation. (2014, January 15). *Bee sensors take flight to help farmers*. Retrieved January 24, 2014, from CSIRO. 10

Databib. (2013). *Databib*. Retrieved January 2, 2014, from Databib: http://databib.org/. 15

Davidoff, F. and Florance, V. (2000). The Informationist: A New Health Profession? *Annals of Internal Medicine*, 132 (12), 996-998. DOI: 10.7326/0003-4819-132-12-200006200-00012. 7, 25

Dewey, B. I. (2004). The Embedded Librarian: Strategic Campus Collaborations. *Resource Sharing and Information Networks*, 17 (1-2), 5-17. DOI: 10.1300/J121v17n01_02. 6

Digital Curation Centre. (2013). *DMPonline*. Retrieved from http://www.dcc.ac.uk/dmponline. 22

ESRI. (2014). *GIS in Libraries*. Retrieved January 24, 2014, from ESRI: http://www.esri.com/industries/libraries/business/libraries. 29

Fields, E. (2010). A unique Twitter use for reference services. *Library Hi Tech News*, 27 (6-7), 14-15. DOI: 10.1108/07419051011095863. 6

Florance, V. (2013). Informationist Careers for Librarians–A Brief History of NLM's Involvement. *Journal of eScience Librarianship*, 2 (1). DOI: 10.7191/jeslib.2013.1040. 29

Functional Genomics Data Society. (2010). Minimum Information About a Microarray Experiment—MIAME 2.0. Retrieved November 6, 2013, from http://www.mged.org/Workgroups/MIAME/miame_2.0.html. 22

Grassian, E. and Trueman, R. B. (2007). Stumbling, bumbling, teleporting and flying ... librarian avatars in Second Life. *Reference Services Review*, 35 (1), 84-89. DOI: 10.1108/00907320710729373. 6

Gray, J. (2009). Jim Gray on eScience: A Transformed Scientific Method. In T. Hey, S. Tansley, & K. Tolle (Eds.), *The Fourth Paradigm: Data-Intensive Scientific Discovery* (pp. xvii-xxxi). Redmond, WA: Microsoft Research. 2

Hall, R. A. (2008). The "embedded" librarian in a freshman speech class: Information literacy instruction in action. *College and Research Libraries News*. 7

Houghton, B. and Rich, E. C. (2001). The Informationist. *Annals of Internal Medicine*, 134 (3), 251-252. DOI: 10.7326/0003-4819-134-3-200102060-00024. 8

Housewright, R., Schonfeld, R. C., and Wulfson, K. (2013). *U.S. Faculty Survey 2012*. Ithaka S+R. 5

iSchools. (2012). *Motivation*. Retrieved January 24, 2014, from iSchools: http://ischools.org/about/history/motivation/. 27

Kearly, J. P. and Phillips, L. (2004). Embedding Library Reference Services in Online Courses. *Internet Reference Services Quarterly*, 9 (1-2), 65-76. DOI: 10.1300/J136v09n01_06. 6

Kelley, M. (2011, October 27). *Major Medical Library Closing Its Doors to Patrons and Moving to Digital Model*. Retrieved November 3, 2013, from The Digital

Shift: http://www.thedigitalshift.com/2011/10/research/major-medical-library-closing-its-doors-to-patrons-and-moving-to-digital-model/. 5

Kessler, S. (2013, January 4). *Inside the Library of Congress's Mission to Organize 170 Billion Tweets*. Retrieved January 24, 2014, from Fast Company: http://www.fastcompany.com/person/robert-dizard. 10

Kim, B. (2013, May). *Keeping Up With... Gamification*. Retrieved January 24, 2014, from Association of College and Research Libraries: http://www.ala.org/acrl/publications/keeping_up_with/gamification. 29

Kronenfeld, M. (2000). "The informationist: a new health profession?" So what are we? Chopped liver? *National Network*, 25 (2), 15. 7

Lamar Soutter Library, University of Massachusetts Medical School and the George C. Gordon Library, Worcester Polytechnic Institute. (2012, February). *Frameworks for a Data Management Curriculum: Course plans for data management instruction to undergraduate and graduate students in science, health science s, and engineering programs*. Retrieved January 2, 2014, from http://library.umassmed.edu/data_management_frameworks.pdf. 17

Matthew, V. and Schroeder, A. (2006). The Embedded Librarian Program. *EDUCAUSE Quarterly* (4), 61-65. 6

Miller, C. M., Rindflesch, T. C., Fiszman, M., Hristovski, D., Shin, D., Rosemblat, G., et al. (2012). A Closed Literature-Based Discovery Technique Finds a Mechanistic Link Between Hypogonadism and Diminished Sleep Quality in Aging Men. *Sleep*, 35 (2), 279-285. DOI: 10.5665/sleep.1640. 24

National Center for Biotechnology Information. (2013, April 1). *GenBank Overview*. Retrieved October 12, 2013, from GenBank: http://www.ncbi.nlm.nih.gov/genbank/. 24

National Institutes of Health. (2007). *NIH Data Sharing Policy*. Retrieved from http://grants.nih.gov/grants/policy/data_sharing/. 22

National Institutes of Health. (2013). *NIH Public Access Policy Details*. Retrieved November 8, 2013, from http://publicaccess.nih.gov/policy.htm. 19, 23

National Science Foundation. (2011). *Dissemination and Sharing of Research Results*. Retrieved from http://www.nsf.gov/bfa/dias/policy/dmp.jsp. 22

National Science Foundation. (2012, October 4). *Issuance of a new NSF Proposal & Award Policies and Procedures Guide*. Retrieved 3 2014, January , from National Science Foundation: http://www.nsf.gov/pubs/2013/nsf13004/nsf13004.jsp. 20

Perlis, R. H., Iosifescu, D. V., Castro, V. M., Murphy, S. N., Gainer, V. S., Minnier, J., et al. (2012). Using electronic medical records to enable large-scale studies in psychiatry: treatment resistant depression as a model. *Psychological Medicine*, 42 (1), 41-50. DOI: 10.1017/S0033291711000997. 25

Priem, J., Taraborelli, D., Groth, P., and Neylon, C. (2010, October 26). *Altmetrics: a manifesto*. Retrieved January 24, 2014, from altmetrics: http://altmetrics.org/manifesto/. 29

Purdue University Libraries. (2012). *Data Curation Profiles Toolkit*. Retrieved October 24, 2013, from http://datacurationprofiles.org. 15, 26

Reference and User Services Association. (2008, January 14). *Definitions of Reference*. Retrieved December 12, 2013, from Reference and User Services Association (RUSA): http://www.ala.org/rusa/resources/guidelines/definitionsreference. 13

Reference and User Services Association Task Force on Professional Competencies. (2003, January 26). *Professional Competencies for Reference and User Services Librarians*. Retrieved September 12, 2013, from American Library Association: http://www.ala.org/rusa/resources/guidelines/professional. 14, 21

Sandroni, S. (2001). The Informationist. *Annals of Internal Medicine*, 134 (3), 251. DOI: 10.7326/0003-4819-134-3-200102060-00023. 8

Shumaker, D. and Tally, M. (2010). Models of embedded librarianship: A research summary. *Information Outlook*, 14 (1), 26-35. 7

Tenopir, C., Allard, S., Douglass, K., Aydinoglu, A. U., Wu, L., Read, E., et al. (2011, June 29). Data Sharing by Scientists: Practices and Perceptions. *PLoS ONE*. DOI: 10.1371/journal.pone.0021101. 23

The Knowledge Network for Biocomplexity. (n.d.). *Ecological Metadata Language (EML)*. Retrieved November 1, 2013, from http://knb.ecoinformatics.org/software/eml/. 22

University of California. (2013). *UC Open Access Policy*. Retrieved September 20, 2013, from Office of Scholarly Communication: http://osc.universityofcalifornia.edu/open-access-policy/. 23

University of California Curation Center. (2013). *DMPTool*. Retrieved from https://dmp.cdlib.org/. 22

Zhao, S., Prenger, K., Smith, L., Messina, T., Fan, H., Jaeger, E., et al. (2013). Rainbow: a tool for large-scale whole-genome sequencing data analysis using cloud computing. *BMC Genomics*, 14. DOI: 10.1186/1471-2164-14-425. 11